The Tales of Hans Andersen

Dramatized by Pete Meakin
From the stories by Hans Christian Andersen

Samuel French — London
New York - Toronto - Hollywood

© 2003 BY PETE MEAKIN

Rights of Performance by Amateurs are controlled by Samuel French Ltd, 52 Fitzroy Street, London W1T 5JR, and they, or their authorized agents, issue licences to amateurs on payment of a fee. **It is an infringement of the Copyright to give any performance or public reading of the play before the fee has been paid and the licence issued.**
The Royalty Fee indicated below is subject to contract and subject to variation at the sole discretion of Samuel French Ltd.

Basic fee for each and every
performance by amateurs   Code L
in the British Isles

The Professional Rights in this play are controlled by SAMUEL FRENCH LTD.

The publication of this play does not imply that it is necessarily available for performance by amateurs or professionals, either in the British Isles or Overseas. Amateurs and professionals considering a production are strongly advised in their own interests to apply to the appropriate agents for written consent before starting rehearsals or booking a theatre or hall.

ISBN 0 573 05131 3

Please see page vi for further copyright information.

TALES OF HANS ANDERSEN

First performed by the Derby Playhouse Youth Theatre at the Derby Playhouse on 11th April 2001, with the following cast:

Ball	Rachel Allsopp
Chorus	Joanna Applewhite
Cook	Merryn Ashwell
Chorus/Clarinet	Holly Bertalan
Chorus	Lauren Bird
Robber Girl	Katrina Bleach-Lawrence
Chorus	Lucy Bramley
Wild Raven	Morgan Brind
Chorus	Kelsey Brookfield
Servant	Katie Burns
Swallow	Holly Burrows
Chorus	Lauren Calladine
Adult Kay	Phil Carter
Chorus	Rajpreet Chima
Dancer	Isabelle Cox
Chorus	Sarah Dennis
Chorus	Philippa Dunn
Chorus	Lizzie Dutton
Chorus	Reece Edwards
Chorus	Lucie Ellis
Tin Soldier 4	Andrew Faley
"Little Match Girl" Boy	Sam Fearn
Water Rat	Laura Fovargue
Chorus/violin	Helena Franklin
Chorus	Emma Gerrard
Chorus	Jessica Goddard
Tin Soldier 8/Bell Lyre	Andrew Harker
Princess	Vicky Harrison
Tin Soldier 3	Tim Hart
1st Wood Pigeon	Eve Hedderwick Turner
Tin Soldier 10	Sam Hockey
Tin Soldier 11	Thomas Holding
Chorus	Lucy Holmes
Sunshine	Daniel Hufton

Chorus	Vickie Irish
Brave Tin Soldier	Michael Jones
Chorus	Rebecca Kelly
Bae	Nick Kennedy
Prince/Bell Lyre	Kit Latham
Chorus	Victoria Laverick
Sorcerer	Richard Law
Tin Soldier 7	James Littlewood
Tin Soldier 6	Simon Llanos
Chorus	Laura Lomas
Old Grandmother	Alex Maher
Chorus/Flute	Alistair Massey
Robber Woman	Lucy McCormick
Chorus/Drum	David Mendham
Chorus	Sarah Middleton
Chorus	Carl Miller
Chorus	Alann Millin
Enchantress/Cornet	Claire Milner
Father	Michael Norledge
Whipping Top	Jonathan O'Boyle
"Brave Tin Soldier" Boy	Darryl Palmer
Chorus	Rachael Parker
Chorus	Sarah Parker
Little Match Girl	Charlotte Peat
Swallow	Daisy Pettinger
Chorus/Clarinet	Chloe Poplar
Tin Soldier 9	Thomas Powis
Gerda	Victoria Pym
Chorus	Katherine Ray
Tame Raven	Cleo Reeves
2nd Wood Pigeon	Victoria Robinson
1st Boy	Simon Roe
Tin Soldier 5	Michael Seymour
Grandmother	Bethany Sheldon
Fish	Tom Shirly
Chorus	Laura Smith
Chorus	Lizzie Smith
Sophy/Adult Gerda	Katie Stannard
Tin Soldier 2	Chris Suckling
Chorus/Violin	Melanie Sykens
Chorus	Ben Taylor
Chorus	Mark Tomlin
Tin Soldier 1	Luke Walker
2nd Boy	Keith Wallis

Kay	Sam Weatherald
Imp	Dean Whatton
Chorus	Georgina Wild
Nutcracker/Violin	Bethan Wiley
Chorus/Violin	Megan Wiley
Rose Tree	Beth Williams
Snow Queen	Lizzie Winkler
Chorus	Chloe Woodhouse
Humpty Dumpty	Andrew Woods
Chorus	Lucy Woolhouse

Directed by Pete Meakin and Tony Coffey
Original music composed by Tony Coffey
Designed by Andy Miller
Musical direction by Tony Coffey
Movement by Fiona Shelton

COPYRIGHT INFORMATION

(See also page ii)

This play is fully protected under the Copyright Laws of the British Commonwealth of Nations, the United States of America and all countries of the Berne and Universal Copyright Conventions.

All rights including Stage, Motion Picture, Radio, Television, Public Reading, and Translation into Foreign Languages, are strictly reserved.

No part of this publication may lawfully be reproduced in ANY form or by any means — photocopying, typescript, recording (including video-recording), manuscript, electronic, mechanical, or otherwise—or be transmitted or stored in a retrieval system, without prior permission.

Licences for amateur performances are issued subject to the understanding that it shall be made clear in all advertising matter that the audience will witness an amateur performance; that the names of the authors of the plays shall be included on all programmes; and that the integrity of the authors' work will be preserved.

The Royalty Fee is subject to contract and subject to variation at the sole discretion of Samuel French Ltd.

In Theatres or Halls seating Four Hundred or more the fee will be subject to negotiation.

In Territories Overseas the fee quoted above may not apply. A fee will be quoted on application to our local authorized agent, or if there is no such agent, on application to Samuel French Ltd, London.

VIDEO-RECORDING OF AMATEUR PRODUCTIONS

Please note that the copyright laws governing video-recording are extremely complex and that it should not be assumed that any play may be video-recorded for whatever purpose without first obtaining the permission of the appropriate agents. The fact that a play is published by Samuel French Ltd does not indicate that video rights are available or that Samuel French Ltd controls such rights.

CHARACTERS

(Please see Author's Notes on page ix and notes on doubling on page x)

Narrators	First Boy
Little Match Girl	Second Boy
Boy	Boat
Walls	Stone Bridge
Father	Water Rat
Big Iron Stove	Fish
Grandmother	Cook
Brave Tin Soldier Boy	Sorcerer
Tin Soldier 1	Gerda
Tin Soldier 2	Kay
Tin Soldier 3	Old Grandmother
Tin Soldier 4	Snow Queen
Tin Soldier 5	Sunshine
Tin Soldier 6	1st Swallow
Tin Soldier 7	2nd Swallow
Tin Soldier 8	Enchantress
Tin Soldier 9	Rose-tree
Tin Soldier 10	Wild Raven
Tin Soldier 11	Tame Raven
Brave Tin Soldier	Prince
Nutcracker	Princess
Whipping Top	Robber Woman
Ball	Robber Girl
Humpty Dumpty	Bae
Sophy	1st Wood Pigeon
Trees	2nd Wood Pigeon
Swans	Adult Kay
Dancer	Adult Gerda
Imp	
Servant	

SYNOPSIS OF SCENES

Act I
THE LITTLE MATCH GIRL
THE BRAVE TIN SOLDIER

Act II
THE SNOW QUEEN

MUSIC NOTES

The play contains music cues and there are sections of poems by Alfred, Lord Tennyson, William Blake and Hans Christian Andersen included as songs. Please see Author's Notes regarding the original score on page ix. The use of this music is not mandatory, but there may be an additional fee payable.

If using any copyright music other than Tony Coffey's score (see p. xi) please read the note below

---

A licence issued by Samuel French Ltd to perform this play does not include permission to use any Incidental music specified in this copy. Where the place of performance is already licensed by the PERFORMING RIGHT SOCIETY a return of the music used must be made to them. If the place of performance is not so licensed then application should be made to the Performing Right Society, 29 Berners Street, London W1.

A separate and additional licence from PHONOGRAPHIC PERFORMANCES LTD, 1 Upper James Street, London W1R 3HG is needed whenever commercial recordings are used.

AUTHOR'S NOTES

Casting requirements
This dramatization contains, essentially, two types of part which can be divided up between as few as 10 actors or as many as 100 (or more). The two types are: (1) named characters and (2) numbered characters. The named characters are basically delivered in character, and the numbered characters are essentially narrators. The numbered speeches (1,2,3, etc.) can literally be apportioned to anyone who happens to be on stage at that particular time and who is currently not a named character. (In the original production by the Derby Playhouse Youth Theatre, most of the cast were on stage for most of the time.) The minimum number of actors and the parts they would each need to play are detailed on page x.

Design
The original set design – by Andy Miller – was very simple but also very effective. In essence, it was a "black box" containing a number of "life-size" children's wooden building bricks which the cast arranged to form the various locations, houses, vessels, and so on. The Sorcerer's Mirror and the Snow Queen's Ice Palace were simply formed by lengths of rope. Costumes were extremely basic with the cast utilizing coloured squares of materials of various sizes to form shawls, cloaks, handkerchiefs (for the flowers), and so on. Props were also minimal: twigs for the Little Match Girl's matches, sticks of wood for the Tin Soldiers' rifles, etc.

Original music
The original music for the Derby Playhouse production was composed and orchestrated by Tony Coffey with the cast members themselves playing a variety of instruments including bell-lyres, violins, flutes, drums, cornet, oboe and clarinets.

If required, the original score can be hired from Tony Coffey, c/o Derby Playhouse, Theatre Walk, Eagle Centre, Derby DE1 2NF.

Pete Meakin

NOTES ON DOUBLING
For Cast of Ten
(5 Male, 5 Female)

Actor 1 (Female): Little Match Girl, Tree 1, Servant, Boat, 1st Swallow, Rose-tree, Princess, Robber Girl.

Actor 2 (Male): "Little Match Girl" Boy, Tin Soldier, Imp, Stone Bridge 1, Sorcerer, Bae.

Actor 3 (Female): Stage Right Wall 1, Christmas Tree, Grandmother, Tree 2, Cook, 2nd Swallow, Tame Raven.

Actor 4 (Male): Stage Right Wall 2, Father, Christmas Tree, "Brave Tin Soldier" Boy, Humpty Dumpty, Wild Raven.

Actor 5 (Female): Stage Left Wall 1, Christmas Tree, Sophy, Stone Bridge 2, Snow Queen.

Actor 6 (Male): Stage Left Wall 2, Christmas Tree, Tin Soldier, First Boy, Kay, Adult Kay.

Actor 7 (Female): Big Iron Stove 1, Nutcracker, Dancer, Old Grandmother, Enchantress, Robber Woman.

Actor 8 (Male): Big Iron Stove 2, Tin Soldier, Whipping Top, Second Boy, Fish, 1st Wood Pigeon.

Actor 9 (Female): Ball, Swans, Water Rat, Gerda.

Actor 10 (Male): Brave Tin Soldier, Sunshine, Prince, 2nd Wood Pigeon.

Please note: if the play is to be performed by as few as ten performers, then there will only be three Tin Soldiers, not including the Brave Tin Soldier himself, and the eleven Tin Soldiers parts as written will have to be divided up between the three.

ACT I

The Little Match Girl

In the original, there was a show-cloth with the title of the Little Match Girl emblazoned on the front

There are a number of coloured life-sized children's wooden building blocks. These remain on stage throughout the play and are manipulated by the cast to create each new setting

As a general rule-of-thumb, the Narrators responsible for describing the new scene are also responsible for constructing the new arrangement of blocks. This way the audience's attention is not drawn away from the narration towards some extraneous and distracting activity

Rather than the blocks being used literally to create the rooms in which the action takes place, the Chorus will use a combination of their own bodies and the blocks to create certain aspects of the room or house in which the room is located

Props, wherever possible, should be taken out of the boxes or out of the actor's pockets. This has the effect of helping to make the production "self-contained" à la magicians or travelling entertainers

Snow is falling and music plays

Narrator 1 enters

Narrator 1 It was snowing ...

Narrator 2 enters

Narrator 2 It was dreadfully cold ...

Narrator 3 enters

Narrator 3 And darkness was falling on the last evening of the year ...

Narrator 1
Narrator 2 (*together*) New Year's Eve.
Narrator 3

The music stops

>*The Little Match Girl enters, wearing an old apron and carrying a wooden box of matches*

Little Match Girl And in this cold and darkness, a poor little girl with bare feet and nothing on her head was walking along the street. She had been wearing slippers when she left home ...
Narrator 1
Narrator 2 (*together*) But they were very big slippers.
Narrator 3
Little Match Girl Her mother had been the last to use them, and they were so big that the little girl had lost them when hurrying across the street, as two carriages had been driving by at an awful speed.
Narrator 1 One of the slippers was nowhere to be seen ...

>*A Boy enters, waving a large slipper*

Boy And a boy ran off with the other, saying, (*to the Little Match Girl*) I can use this as a cradle when I have children of my own. Thanks!

>*He exits*

Narrator 2 So now the little girl was walking along on tiny bare feet that were red and blue with cold.
Little Match Girl She was holding a bundle of matches in her old apron, and she had some in her hand.
Narrator 3 No-one had bought any from her all day long.
Narrator 2 No-one had given her a penny ...
Narrator 1 And hungry and chilled to the bone ...
Little Match Girl She walked along looking very sad.
Narrator 1 The white snowflakes were falling on her long black hair that curled beautifully around her neck ...
Little Match Girl But she scarcely gave it a thought.
Narrator 2 In all the windows candles were shining, and there was a lovely smell of roast turkey in the street.
Narrator 1
Narrator 2 (*together*) It was New Year's Eve ...
Narrator 3

Act I, The Little Match Girl

Little Match Girl And that was something to which she did give a thought ...

The Chorus enter; singing. During the song, they divide into two groups and using the stage blocks, form the walls of two houses with a corner niche in between

Chorus Ring out the old, ring in the new,
Ring, happy bells, across the snow;
The year is going, let him go;
Ring out the false, ring in the true.

Ring out, wild bells, to the wild sky,
The flying cloud, the frosty light;
The year is dying in the night;
Ring out, wild bells, and let him die.
[*Alfred, Lord Tennyson*]

Little Match Girl In a corner between two houses ...
Stage Right Wall One of them sticking a little further into the street than the other ...
Little Match Girl The little girl sat down and huddled up.
Stage Left Wall She pulled her legs up under her ...
Little Match Girl But she became even colder.
Stage Right Wall And she didn't dare go home ...
Little Match Girl Because she hadn't sold any matches or received a single penny.

The Father steps out from the wall

Father Her father would beat her.
Little Match Girl And besides it was cold at home, too.

Narrator 4 steps out from the wall

Narrator 4 Then she thought that a little match might help a bit. If only she dared take one from the bundle, strike it against the wall and warm her fingers. She pulled one out ...

The Little Match Girl takes a match and strikes the match against the Stage Right Wall

Chorus (*as she strikes the match*) Pshshsh!!
Stage Right Wall How it spluttered!

Stage Left Wall How it burned!
Narrator 3 It was a warm, clear flame, just like a candle when she held her hand around it, and a curious candle it was.
Little Match Girl It seemed to the little girl that she was sitting in front of ——

Two members of the Chorus, using appropriate blocks, form a big iron stove. A tall cylindrical block can be used and the actors' fists can be the knobs. There is a bar of magical music

Big Iron Stove A big iron stove

There is a bar of magical music

And the fire was burning ——
Chorus Divinely.

There is a bar of magical music

Little Match Girl It gave out a wonderful warmth ...
Stage Right Wall ⎫
Stage Left Wall ⎬ (*together*) But then the flame — died.

There is a bar of disappointed music

Big Iron Stove And the stove ——
Chorus — vanished.

There is a bar of disappointed music. The big iron stove vanishes and the two actors reform themselves back into the wall

Little Match Girl There she sat with a little stump of the burned-out match in her hand.

Narrator 5 steps forward

Narrator 5 She struck a fresh match.

The Little Match Girl strikes a match on the Stage Left Wall

Chorus (*as she does*) Pshshsh!!
Narrator 5 It burned brightly. And the wall became ——
Stage Left Wall — transparent

Act I, The Little Match Girl

The Stage Left Wall starts to move and splits into two

Stage Left Wall 1 Like a piece of gauze.

The Stage Left Wall continues to move

Stage Left Wall 2 Where the glow from the match shone on it.
Little Match Girl She could see straight into the parlour, where the table was laid with a shining white cloth and fine porcelain. And there was ——
Stage Right Wall A roast turkey!

The Stage Left Wall group themselves together to form a turkey

Stage Left Wall Gobble, gobble.
Stage Left Wall 1 Stuffed with prunes.
Stage Left Wall 2 And apples.
Stage Left Walls (*together*) Oh, no!
Stage Right Wall Gobble, gobble, gobble!
Little Match Girl Then the match went out.
Stage Left Wall And there was nothing to be seen but the thick, cold wall.
Little Match Girl She lit another match. (*She lights another match*)
Stage Right Wall ⎱ (*together*) Pshshsh!! Then she was sitting under the
Stage Left Wall ⎰ loveliest Christmas tree.

The Chorus begin to hum. Stage Left Wall and Stage Right Wall cluster together to form the base of a Christmas tree

Other Chorus members enter, carrying lanterns. Using variations in height, they are able to form the up-turned cone-shape of a Christmas tree

Little Match Girl Which was even bigger and more gloriously decorated than the one she had once seen through the glass door at the house of a rich merchant.

The Chorus stops humming

Christmas Tree Thousands of candles were burning on the green branches, and many-coloured ornaments like those decorating the shop windows were looking down on her.
Little Match Girl The little child stretched out both her hands — and then the match went out.

Chorus start to move us *and apart from one another*

Chorus But all the Christmas candles rose higher and higher until she could see that they were the night stars.

The Little Match Girl starts to move forward

Little Match Girl One of them fell ...
Chorus Making a long fiery streak in the sky.

The Chorus whistle as they watch the imagined falling star descend over the audience

Little Match Girl Someone's dying, said the little girl. Her old grandmother, who was the only person ever to have been kind to her, but who was dead now, had said that when a star falls, a soul is on its way up to God. She struck another match. (*She strikes a match*)
Chorus Pshshsh!!
Little Match Girl It shone all around, and in the glow ——

The Grandmother enters

Grandmother —— stood her old grandmother, so clear, so radiant, gentle and sublime.
Little Match Girl Grandma! Shouted the little girl. Oh, take me with you. I know you'll have gone when the match goes out — gone like the warm stove, the lovely roast turkey and the wonderful big Christmas tree! She hurried to strike the rest of the matches in the bundle, because she wanted to keep her grandmother. (*She strikes the rest of her matches*)
Chorus Pshshsh!! Pshshsh!! Pshshsh!!
Little Match Girl And the matches shone with such radiance that it was brighter than daylight.

There is music

Grandmother Never before had grandmother seemed so beautiful. She lifted the little girl up in her arms, and in radiance and joy they flew ——

The Little Match Girl's hands come together with the Grandmother's hands. During the following, they fly to "Heaven" by retreating us. *The two are enveloped by the rest of the Chorus, so that the Grandmother can join as a member of the Chorus and the Little Match Girl can lie dead unseen*

Little Match Girl
Grandmother } (*together*) — so high.

Act I, The Little Match Girl 7

Chorus Ever so high.
Narrator 6 Now there was no cold.
Narrator 7 No hunger.
Narrator 8 No fear.
Narrator 6
Narrator 7 (*together*) They were with —
Narrator 8
Chorus — God.
(*Singing*) He doth give his joy to all,
He becomes an infant small.
He becomes a man of woe,
He doth feel the sorrow too.

Think not thou canst sigh a sigh,
And thy maker is not by;
Think not thou canst weep a tear,
And thy maker is not near.

Oh, he gives to us his joy
That our grief he may destroy;
Till our grief is fled and gone,
He doth sit by us and moan.
[*William Blake*]

(*Speaking*) New Year's Day!

All the Chorus exit, with the exception of Narrators 9 and 10

The body of the Little Match Girl still holding her wooden box is revealed.
Narrator 9 walks towards the body of the Little Match Girl

Narrator 9 But in the corner near the house in that cold morning hour lay the little girl with red cheeks and a smile on her lips — frozen to death on the last evening of the old year.
Narrator 10 (*stepping forward*) New Year's morning dawned over the little body sitting there with the matches —(*s/he sees the box of matches*) of which almost all had been burned.
Narrator 9 She must have wanted to warm herself.
Narrator 10 Some people said. No-one knew what beautiful things she had seen —(*s/he places the Little Match Girl's box* DC) or in what radiance she and her grandmother had entered into the joy of the New Year.

The Chorus enter

Chorus (*singing*) Ring out the grief that saps the mind,
For those that here we see no more;
Ring out the feud of rich and poor,
Ring in redress to all mankind.

Ring out the want, the care, the sin,
The faithless coldness of the times;
Ring out, ring out thy mournful rhymes,
But ring the fuller minstrel in.
[*Alfred, Lord Tennyson*]

Black-out

THE BRAVE TIN SOLDIER

There is a show-cloth with the title of the tale emblazoned on the front. The wooden box remains DS

The Chorus hum the tune of "Happy Birthday"

The "Brave Tin Soldier" Boy (BTS Boy) enters and takes the lid off the wooden box, previously belonging to the Little Match Girl

The Chorus stop humming. A fanfare plays

BTS Boy Tin Soldiers!
Chorus Tin Soldiers!

The Boy takes out toy tin soldiers from the box and begins to stand them in a line. A military drum and a cornet are heard. Twelve (or as many/as few as you wish) Tin Soldiers emerge from the Chorus. They carry muskets. They form a line and mirror the toy soldiers

Tin Soldier 3 There was once a box of tin soldiers.
Tin Soldier 9 Who were all brothers.
Tin Soldier 6 For they were made out of the same old tin spoon.
Tin Soldier 1 They looked straight before them.
Tin Soldier 5 Shouldering their muskets in military style. Hup!

The Soldiers shoulder their muskets

Tin Soldier 10 And their uniforms were blue.
Tin Soldier 11 And red.

Act I, The Brave Tin Soldier   9

Tin Soldiers (*together*) Of the most splendid description.

The Boy stands the final toy soldiers up

BTS Boy Tin Soldiers!
Tin Soldier 4 Were the very first words they heard in this world.
Tin Soldier 8 When the lid was taken off the box in which they lay.
Tin Soldier 2 That was the exclamation of the little boy who had received them as a birthday present.
Tin Soldier 7 One soldier was the very image of the other.

The Brave Tin Soldier limps forward from the Chorus. One of his legs is shrivelled and cannot support his weight

Brave Tin Soldier With the exception of a single one, who had only one proper leg, for he had been cast last, when there was not enough tin remaining. But he stood as firmly on his one sound leg as the others on their two.
BTS Boy At night all the people of the house went to bed. (*He makes towards the exit*) Coming, Mother!

The BTS Boy exits

Chorus Now the playthings began to play …

Music plays. The Chorus mould themselves into various playthings — nutcrackers, balls, whipping tops and Humpty Dumpty, etc. There is a cacophonous commotion as the playthings play

Nutcracker The nutcracker turned somersaults.

The Nutcracker turns somersaults. The Chorus applaud. A Whipping Top comes forward

Whipping Top The Whipping Top ——

A Ball comes forward from the chorus

Ball — said to the Ball.
Whipping Top Shall we be married, as we live in the same box?
Ball But the Ball, who wore a dress of Moroccan leather, and thought as much of herself as any other young lady, would not even condescend to reply. Hum!

Whipping Top Look at me, said the Top to the Ball. What do you say now? Shall we be engaged to each other? We should suit each other so well — you spring and I spin. No-one could be happier than we should be.
Ball Indeed! Do you think so? Perhaps you do not know that my father and mother were Moroccan Slippers, and that I have a Spanish cork in my body?
Whipping Top Yes; but I am made of mahogany, said the Top. The Mayor himself turned me.
Ball Can I believe it? Asked the Ball.
Whipping Top May I never be whipped again, said the Top, if I am not telling the truth.
Ball You certainly know how to speak for yourself very well, said the Ball, but, I cannot accept your proposal. I am almost engaged to a Swallow. Every time I fly up in the air, he puts his head out of the nest and says, will you? And I have said yes, to myself silently, and that is as good as being half engaged. But I will promise never to forget you.
Whipping Top Much good that will be to me, said the Top.
Whipping Top
Ball } (*together*) And they spoke to each other no more.

There is music. There is a cacophonous commotion as the playthings play

Narrator 11 There was now a knocking from a box ——

A knocking is heard

—— where the beautiful doll, Sophy, was standing alone.

Humpty Dumpty steps forward

Humpty Dumpty And Humpty Dumpty, jumping on to the table, lay flat down, and crept as near as possible to the edge without falling off.

Sophy steps out from a wooden building block

Sophy Then Sophy stepped out and looked around her, quite astonished. I should like to dance! She said.
Humpty Dumpty Will you dance with me? Humpty Dumpty asked.
Sophy Oh, my! You're a pretty fellow to dance, she said, and turned her back upon him. She then seated herself upon the table, expecting that one of the Tin Soldiers would come and engage her.
Tin Soldiers (*together*) But none came.
Sophy And then she coughed, hem, hem, hem!

Act I, The Brave Tin Soldier

Tin Soldiers (*together*) But none came for all that.

Humpty Dumpty And as no-one would dance with Humpty Dumpty, he decided to sing a sad song instead:

    (*Singing*)   Oh, were I rich! That fervent wish, in truth,
                    Was very often mine in early youth.
                      Oh, were I rich! A soldier I'd be,
                      With musket and uniform so brave and free!

                      Did she but know my longings — No, hope dies,
                      For still to silence I am doomed as ever,
                      Let her not feel my torture now nor never!
                      La la ... La la ... la laaaa

                      Oh, were I rich! So sounds to heaven my prayer:
                      I've watched that girl grow up so tall and fair,
                      She is so good, so pretty, and so wise,
                      Could she but read my heart with those dear eyes,

The Chorus join in singing on the La

                      Did she but know my longings — No, hope dies,
                      For still to silence I am doomed as ever,
                      Let her not feel my torture now nor never!
                      La la ... La la ... la laaaa
                      [*Hans Christian Andersen*]

Narrator 10 There were many other playthings in the nursery as well.

Narrator 11 But that which caught the eye the most was a pretty castle made of cardboard.

Music plays. The Chorus make a castle using the blocks. This can be constructed with two columns of blocks with Chorus members playing the windows

Narrator 12 wanders around the castle

Narrator 12 One could see through the windows into the rooms.

Members of the Chorus mould their bodies to become trees. They take a piece of rope that will represent a lake and stand before it

Trees And in front there were several small trees.

Narrator 12 Standing round a piece of mirror, which represented a lake.

Other members of the Chorus mould their bodies to become swans on the represented lake

Swans Reflecting the wax swans that swam upon it.
Narrator 13 It was all pretty, but the prettiest of all was a little girl, who stood in the middle of the open door.

A Dancer comes from the Chorus

Dancer She was also made of cardboard, but had a dress of the thinnest muslin, and a piece of blue ribbon across her shoulders fastened with a brooch quite as big as her whole face. The little girl held both her arms stretched out, for she was a dancer.
Brave Tin Soldier And one leg was raised so high that the Tin Soldier could not see it, so that he thought she, like himself, had only one good leg. That would be just the wife for me, he thought, but she is rather grand, living in a castle, whereas I have only a box, and even that I have to share with other Tin Soldiers. That is no place for her; but yet I must try to make acquaintance with her. So he laid himself down flat beside the castle — from where he could watch the pretty lady.
Dancer Who began to dance.
Brave Tin Soldier And the Brave Tin Soldier did not turn his eyes from her for one instant

Music plays. The Dancer dances. The Chorus make the sound of a clock striking, bringing the dance to an abrupt halt

Chorus It now struck twelve.

The clock continues to strike twelve

Narrator 11 And all of a sudden — the lid flew off the snuff box.

The lid flies off one of the blocks and out pops the Little Imp

Chorus Aaaaaaaagggghhhh!!!!
Imp Ha! Ha! Ha! Ha! Ha! But it was not snuff that was in the box. Oh, no. It was a little Imp.
Chorus Such as children call a *Jack-in-the-box*.
Imp Tin Soldier, said the Imp, keep your eyes to yourself!
Brave Tin Soldier But the Tin Soldier pretended not to hear him.

Act I, The Brave Tin Soldier

Imp Well, you just wait until tomorrow.
Narrator 11 The Imp said; and vanished back into the box.

The Imp vanishes back into the block

Music plays

Narrator 13 The next morning, as soon as the children were up, the Tin Soldier was stood in the window, and it was either the Imp's doing ——
Imp (*from inside the box*) Ha! Ha! Ha! Ha! Ha!
Narrator 13 Or the draught — anyhow, the window flew open ——
Chorus Agh!
Narrator 13 — and the soldier went head over heels from the second storey down into the street.

There is falling music

Narrator 14 That was a dreadful fall, and he reached the ground head first.
Brave Tin Soldier A most undignified position for a soldier.

A Servant enters

Servant The servant ——

The Brave Tin Soldier Boy enters

BTS Boy — and the little Boy came running down immediately to look for it, but ——
Brave Tin Soldier — though they were near treading upon him ——
Servant ⎱ (*together*) — they could not find him.
BTS Boy ⎰

The Servant and the BTS Boy exit

Narrator 15 If the soldier had cried out, here I am!, they would certainly have found him.
Brave Tin Soldier But he did not think it becoming to call out, as he was in uniform.
Chorus It now began to rain.

The Chorus make the sounds of rain falling. This they do vocally and by tapping/drumming on the stage floor

And the drops fell faster.

The drops fall faster

   And faster.

The drops fall faster

   Until it came down in torrents.

The rain comes down in torrents

First Boy steps out of the Chorus

First Boy When the rain was over —

Second Boy steps out of the Chorus

Second Boy — two boys came that way.
First Boy And one of them exclaimed, look, here lies a Tin Soldier! (*He picks up the soldier left by the BTS Boy*)
Second Boy He shall have a sail down the gutter!
First Boy So they made a boat out of a piece of newspaper —

The First Boy makes a paper boat. Some members of the Chorus mirror the boy forming a boat using their bodies and blocks

First Boy — and put it —
Brave Tin Soldier ⎫
Second Boy ⎭ (*together*) — with the Soldier standing in the middle ...

The Second Boy puts the tin soldier into the paper boat as the Brave Tin Soldier goes into the Chorus Boat

First Boy ... into the water ...
Second Boy ... which, after the heavy rain, rushed down the street.
Two Boys (*together*) And the Boys ran by the side, shouting at the Tin Soldier.
Boat Chorus The paperboat was tossed about.

The Boat is tossed about. The Chorus make the sounds of a tempest

Boat Chorus And occasionally whirled round and round.

The Boat whirls round. The Chorus make the sounds of a tempest

Act I, The Brave Tin Soldier

Boat Chorus So that the Soldier quite shook.
Brave Tin Soldier But yet he did not move a feature, looking straight before him and shouldering his musket.
Boat Chorus All at once, the gutter turned under the pavement.

The Boat turns a right angle. Two Chorus members form a Stone Bridge

Stone Bridge Which thus formed a Stone Bridge.
Brave Tin Soldier And here the Soldier was as utterly in darkness as if he were in his box. Where am I going to now? He thought. This is certainly the Imp's doing. But if only that dear little dancer were here in the boat with me, it might be twice as dark for all I'd care.

A Water Rat enters from under the Stone Bridge

Water Rat Now a large Water Rat suddenly appeared, as she lived under the Bridge. Have you a pass? She cried. Come, show your pass!
Brave Tin Soldier But the Tin Soldier was silent, holding his gun still firmer.
Boat The Boat rushed on.
Water Rat And the Rat after it.

The Rat chases after the boat, on the spot, in slow motion

Boat Oh, how it showed its teeth.

The Water Rat shows her teeth

And shouted to the wooden beams and the pieces of straw ...
Water Rat Stop him! Stop him! He has not paid his toll! He has not showed his pass!
Boat The rushing of the water grew stronger and stronger.
Brave Tin Soldier And already the Soldier could see light at the far end.

The Chorus make the distant sounds of rushing water

Brave Tin Soldier But at the same time he heard a noise which might have frightened the bravest man.

The rushing water sounds grow

Narrator 16 Only imagine, where the gutter ended, it emptied itself into ——
Chorus A canal!

The rushing water sounds continue to grow

Brave Tin Soldier He was so near upon it that there was no help.
Boat And down the boat rushed.
Brave Tin Soldier The poor Soldier holding himself as steady as he possibly could. No-one should be able to say that he as much as blinked his eyes!

The rushing water sounds continue to grow. The Boat whirls round

Narrator 16 Three times the boat was whirled round and round, and was filled with water nearly up to the top, so that surely it must sink.
Brave Tin Soldier The water already reached up to the Soldier's shoulders.
Narrator 16 And the boat sank deeper and deeper, and more and more the paper became unfastened.

The water sounds continue. The Chorus Boat begins to break apart

Brave Tin Soldier The water was now over his head. And he thought of the pretty little dancer, whom he should see no more.
Chorus Then the paper tore.

The Boat breaks up completely

Brave Tin Soldier And he fell through.

The sounds and movement stop abruptly

A Fish enters

Fish But at that very moment he was swallowed by a large fish. Gulp!

The Fish exits

The Brave Tin Soldier is enshrouded by all of the Chorus

Narrator 16 Oh, how dark it was! Worse than under the bridge! And there was no room to move.
Brave Tin Soldier (*from inside the Chorus*) But the Tin Soldier's courage did not forsake him.
Narrator 16 He lay there his full length with his musket in his arm.

Narrator 17 breaks away from the Chorus

Narrator 17 Suddenly light appeared.

The Cook enters

Act I, The Brave Tin Soldier   17

Cook And a voice exclaimed, the Tin Soldier!
Narrator 17 The fish had been caught.

Narrator 18 breaks away from the Chorus

Narrator 18 And taken to the market.

Narrator 19 breaks away from the Chorus

Narrator 19 Where it was bought.

Narrator 20 breaks away from the chorus

Narrator 20 And carried into the kitchen.
Cook Where it was cut open with a large knife. With two fingers the Cook took hold of the Soldier and carried him into the room.

The Cook carries the Brave Tin Soldier

Cook So all could see the extraordinary man who had been swallowed by a fish.
Brave Tin Soldier But the Soldier was not at all proud.
Cook He was placed upon the table.
Brave Tin Soldier And wonder of wonders ...

There is a cacophonous commotion as the Chorus reform into the nursery. This includes the line of Tin Soldiers, the castle and a stove like the one formed in the Little Match Girl

The Tin Soldier was in the same room he had been in before.
Castle The beautiful Castle was there.

The Dancer's music plays

   The Dancer enters, dancing

Dancer And the pretty little Dancer.

Dancer's music continues. She dances around the Brave Tin Soldier

   The BTS Boy enters and brings the music to an abrupt halt

BTS Boy Then the Boy took the Soldier and threw him into the fire. (*He throws the toy tin soldier into the stove*)

This is mirrored by the movements of the "human" Brave Tin Soldier as he goes into the stove

Chorus Aaaaaggh!
BTS Boy He didn't know why he had done this.

The Imp jumps out of the box

Chorus Aaaaaggh!
Imp No doubt the Imp had something to do with it. Ha! Ha! Ha! Ha!
Brave Tin Soldier The Tin Soldier stood there in the midst of the flames, and the heat was something dreadful.
Narrator 21 But whether it was the heat of the fire or of his love he did not know.
Brave Tin Soldier His colour had completely gone.
Narrator 21 But whether caused by his travels or by grief, no-one could tell.
Brave Tin Soldier When he felt that he was melting, he looked at the little Dancer.
Dancer And she looked at him.
Brave Tin Soldier And still he stood firmly with his musket at his shoulder.
Chorus Then the door flew open.

The Dancer's music recommences

Dancer And carried away by the draught, the little dancer flew like a sylph into the fire.
Brave Tin Soldier To the Soldier!

The Dancer dances into the fire

Dancer She blazed up.

The music plays on

And was gone.

The music continues

Brave Tin Soldier And the Soldier now melted down into a lump.

The music continues

Chorus The next morning ——

Act I, The Brave Tin Soldier   19

Servant When the Servant cleared out the ashes, she found a tin heart. And a brooch, which was burnt quite black.

Male Chorus (*singing*) Did she but know my longings — No, hope dies,
For still to silence I am doomed as ever,
Let her not feel my torture now nor never!
Female Chorus Did he but know my longings — No, hope dies,
For still to silence I am doomed as ever,
Let him not feel my torture now nor never!
Chorus Did s/he but know my longings — No, hope dies,
For still to silence I am doomed as ever,
Let him/her not feel my torture now nor never!
La la la la laaaa
[*Hans Christian Andersen*]

Black-out

ACT II

The Snow Queen

There is a show-cloth with the title of The Snow Queen on the front

Music plays

The Lights come up on Narrators 22 to 25

Narrator 22 Well, now we are going to begin.
Narrator 23 And when we have got to the end of the story we shall know more than we do now.
Narrator 24 For it is of a wicked sorcerer.
Narrator 22 ⎫
Narrator 23 ⎬ (*together*) One of the very worst sorcerers.
Narrator 24 ⎭

The Narrators raise a mirror made from a rectangle of rope

A Sorcerer enters

Sorcerer One day he was feeling extremely pleased with himself, for he had made a looking-glass which possessed this peculiarity: that everything good or beautiful reflected in it dwindled down to almost nothing. (*He points to a member of the audience*) Like you. But whatever was worthless and unsightly stood out boldly, and became still worse. (*He points to another member of the audience*) Like you.

Narrator 25 comes forward

Narrator 25 Even handsome people became repulsive. (*S/he looks in the mirror and contorts his face to look repulsive*) Or stood on their heads and looked ridiculous. (*S/he stands on her head and looks ridiculous*)
Narrator 24 The faces ——
Narrators (*together*) — were so distorted that they could not be recognized.

All the Narrators pull distorted faces

Narrator 26 enters

Act II, The Snow Queen

Narrator 26 And if anyone had a spot, however small, it was sure to spread over the nose and mouth and face.

Narrator 26 looks into the mirror and distorts his face to look as if the spot is spreading over his nose, mouth and face. Then the spot bursts

Other Narrators Ergh!
Sorcerer That was highly amusing.
Other Narrators The sorcerer said

Narrator 27 enters

Narrator 27 Till at last there was no man and no country that had not been distorted by it.
Narrator 23 Not satisfied with this, they flew up towards heaven with it. But the looking-glass shook so violently that it slipped out of their hands. And fell down to earth.
Narrators Agh!

Narrators move US *with the rope. With each "Agh!" a side of the mirror/rope is pulled out of line with the rest of the rectangle, transforming the mirror/rope into a distorted kind of cat's cradle*

Narrator 23 Agh!

One side of the mirror is pulled

Narrator 22 Agh!

Another side of the mirror is pulled

Narrator 24 Agh!

Another side of the mirror is pulled

Narrator 27 And broke into hundreds of millions of billions of pieces.

Another side of the mirror is pulled

Chorus Agh!

Snow begins to fall

Narrators 28 to 32 enter

Narrator 28 Some of the pieces were no larger than dust and flew about in the air. Whoever got them in their eyes saw the whole human race distorted, for each particle, no matter how small, retained the peculiarity of the whole looking-glass.

Narrator 29 Some people even got a small piece of glass in their hearts, and that was dreadful, for the heart became like a lump of ice.

Narrator 30 Some of the pieces were so large that they were used for panes of window glass; but it would not do to look at one's friends through them.

Narrator 31 puts on spectacles

Narrator 31 Other pieces got made into spectacles. (*To a female member of the audience*) Nice beard, madam.

Narrator 32 And some of the dust of the broken glass is still flying about in the air, as is seen, unfortunately, every day.

The Chorus enter

Chorus   Mercy has a human heart,
               Pity a human face,
               And Love, the human form divine,
               And Peace, the human dress.

               Cruelty has a human heart,
               Jealousy a human face,
               Terror, the human form divine,
               And Secrecy, the human dress.
               [*William Blake*]

The Lights change

A Little Boy and a Little Girl

Narrators 33 to 36 step out of the Chorus

Narrator 33 In a large city, where there were so many people and houses that there was not room enough for all to have a little garden, there lived two poor children.

The Chorus form two houses using the children's building blocks. This can be two cubes, each with a triangular block on the top

   Kay and Gerda enter and sit beside their respective houses

Act II, The Snow Queen 23

Narrator 34 They were not brother and sister, but were as fond of each other as if they had been so.

Narrator 33 (*demonstrating the geography of the place*) Their parents lived exactly opposite in two small attics, for the roof of one house almost joined the other, separated only by the gutter running between them.

Narrator 34 (*also demonstrating*) And one had but to step across the gutter to reach from the one to the other.

Narrator 35 Outside the attic windows, the branches of rose trees bent forward towards each other. (*She produces the rose trees, like bunting from out of the building blocks*) So that it looked almost like a triumphal arch of leaves and flowers.

Narrator 36 The children often received permission to climb out of the windows ——

Kay and Gerda climb through imaginary windows

——and play together underneath the rose trees.

Kay and Gerda play underneath the rose trees

Narrator 37 In winter there was an end to this amusement, for the windows were often frozen quite over. But then the children warmed half-pence on the stove

Kay and Gerda warm half-pence on an imaginary stove

——and laying the warm coin against the frozen glass made a beautiful peep-hole. And behind each round hole there shone a bright sparkling eye.
Gerda That of the little girl.
Kay And the little boy. His name was Kay.
Gerda And hers Gerda.
Narrator 36 In summer. With one jump, they could be together

Kay and Gerda do so

Narrator 37 But in winter ——

It begins to snow

—— they had to run down the many stairs of the one house and up the others.

Kay and Gerda move up and down imaginary stairs

While the snow ——

Chorus — was falling outside.

Kay throws paper snow from out of one of the blocks

The Old Grandmother enters

Old Grandmother The old grandmother said, those are the white bees swarming.
Kay Have they a queen too?
Old Grandmother Yes, they have. She is flying there, where they are swarming the thickest. She is the largest of them all, and never rests quiet on the ground, but flies up again into the black cloud. Often during the winter nights she flies through the streets of the town and looks through the windows, which are then covered with frost, in such strange forms as if they were so many flowers.
Kay Yes, I have seen that!
Gerda Can the Snow Queen come in here?
Kay Let her come! And I will put her on the stove so that she will melt!
Old Grandmother But the Old Grandmother smoothed his hair — (*she smooths Kay's hair*) and told them other stories.

The Old Grandmother exits

Narrator 38 That evening when little Kay was at home and getting ready for bed, he looked through the peep-hole in the window.
Narrator 39 Some flakes of snow were falling, and one amongst them, the very largest, remained lying on the ground.
Narrator 38 It increased more ...
Narrator 38 ⎫
Narrator 39 ⎬ (*together*) And more ...

Narrators 38 and 39 take handfuls of snow from out of their pocket and throw it

The whole Chorus merges together

Chorus And more ...

All the Chorus throw handfuls of snow from out of their pockets into the air

The Snow Queen, dressed in a white cape, enters through this snow

Snow Queen Till at last it became a woman. Dressed in the finest white cape, as if formed by millions of star-like flakes.

Act II, The Snow Queen   25

Kay She was so beautiful.
Snow Queen But of ice — dazzling, glistening ice.
Chorus And yet she was alive.
Snow Queen Her eyes sparkled like two bright stars.
Narrator 38 But they were restless and unsteady.
Snow Queen She nodded towards the window — and beckoned with her finger.
Narrator 39 Which frightened the little boy, so that he jumped away.

Kay jumps away, frightened

Kay And just then it seemed as if a large bird flew past the window.

The Snow Queen exits as a flying bird

Narrator 33 The ——
Narrator 34 — next ——
Narrator 35 — day ——
Narrator 40 It was a clear frost.
Narrator 41 Then came spring.

There is a commotion and flurry of activity, as the Chorus move like the snow

Narrator 42 The sun shone.
Narrator 43 The trees began to bud.
Narrator 44 The swallows built their nests.
Narrator 45 The windows were opened.
Gerda And the little children again sat together.
Kay High up in the gutter on the roof.
Narrator 46 The roses bloomed more beautifully than ever this summer.
Gerda And the little girl had learned a new hymn in which roses were mentioned, reminding her of her own. She sang the hymn to the little boy.
Kay And he joined in.
Gerda
Kay } (*singing*) The rose blooms but its glory past,
                        Christmas then approaches fast.

Kay The little ones held each other by the hand.

Gerda and Kay hold hands

Gerda And kissed the roses.

Gerda and Kay kiss the roses

Kay And stared up into the sky.
Gerda Into the clear sunshine.
Narrator 47 While Kay and Gerda were playing so happily together, the church clock suddenly struck five ——

The Chorus make the sound of a church clock chiming five

And Kay exclaimed ——
Kay Oh, something sharp has flown into my eye! And run into my heart!
Narrator 47 The little girl took him round the neck, and looked into his eye.

Gerda looks into Kay's eye

Gerda No, there is nothing to be seen.
Kay I think it has gone again.
Narrator 47 But it was not gone. It was just one of the pieces of the magic, hateful glass which, you will remember, fell and was broken. Poor Kay had got one of those pieces in his heart, and soon it will become a lump of ice. It no longer hurt him.
Chorus But — it was there.
Kay (*to Gerda*) Why are you crying? It makes you look so ugly and there's nothing the matter with me at all. Look how awful that rose is. (*He tears off one of the roses from the tree*)
Gerda Kay!
Kay It's all worm-eaten. And this one is completely out of shape. (*He tears another rose off*)
Gerda Kay!
Kay They are all ugly flowers.

Kay showers the petals over Gerda and then runs off

Gerda Kay! What on earth is the matter?

The Old Grandmother enters

Old Grandmother Kay would no longer play with Gerda.

The Chorus once again throw handfuls of snow

When winter came and his Old Grandmother tried to tell them stories, he would constantly interrupt her or, when he could manage it, would hide behind her and mimic her most cruelly, so that all who saw it laughed aloud.
Chorus Ha! Ha! Ha! Ha!

Act II, The Snow Queen

Old Grandmother His play was now quite different from what it used to be.

Kay enters

Kay (*sensibly*) It was sensible. One winter's day, when it was snowing, Kay held out his hand and caught some snowflakes. He looked at them through a large magnifying glass. (*He takes out a magnifying-glass and looks at the snow.* To *Gerda*) Look through the glass, Gerda.

Gerda looks through the magnifying-glass

Gerda I have to admit they are quite beautiful, Kay. Like little flowers or ten-cornered stars.
Kay But aren't they more interesting than your real flowers? See there is not a single fault in them. They are perfectly accurate. If only they could remain without melting. Now leave me alone, Gerda. You're making me feel cross.

Gerda exits

The Snow Queen music begins

The Snow Queen enters on a glorious sleigh

Snow Queen (*beckoning to Kay*) Come aboard, little Kay, and we shall go for a splendid ride.

Kay boards the sleigh

But how is it that you are cold? Come, creep under my cloak. (*She covers Kay with her cloak*)
Narrator 48 And she seated him by her side in the sleigh, covering him up with her cloak.
Kay But it seemed to Kay as if he were sinking into a snowdrift.
Snow Queen Are you still cold?
Narrator 48 She asked. And kissed him on the forehead. (*She kisses Kay on the forehead*) Oh, that was colder than ice, and seemed to penetrate to his very heart, which was already half a lump of ice.
Kay He felt as if he were going to die and grew quite frightened. He tried to say his prayers but could think of nothing except his multiplication tables.
Snow Queen The Snow Queen kissed Kay again. (*She kisses Kay on the forehead once more*)

Kay And Kay now began to feel quite comfortable and no longer sensed the cold around him. He completely forgot little Gerda — and all at home.
Snow Queen Now, you must have no more kisses. Or else I shall kiss you to death.
Narrator 48 Kay looked at her.

Kay looks at the Snow Queen

Kay She was so beautiful, and a more intelligent, lovely face he could not imagine. In his eyes she was perfection, and he felt no fear. He told her that he could reckon in his head, and knew the number of square miles in the country as well as the number of its inhabitants.
Snow Queen And she smiled at all he said.

The sleigh, with Kay and the Snow Queen, exits

Narrator 48 And they flew away together. (S/he watches the imagined flight path of the sleigh) High, high, on to the black cloud. They flew over forests and lakes. Beneath them the wolves howled, the snow sparkled, and the cold wind whistled, as if it were singing old songs.

Chorus (*singing*) The rose blooms but its glory past,
　　　　　　Christmas then approaches fast.

There is a lighting change

The Flower Garden of the Enchantress

Gerda enters

Gerda But how did little Gerda fare when Kay did not return? What could have become of him?
Chorus No-one knew.
Narrator 49 No-one could give any information.
Chorus No-one could tell where he was.
Narrator 49 Many tears were shed.
Gerda And little Gerda cried more than all.
Narrator 49 It was then said that he was ——
Chorus — *dead*.
Narrator 49 That he had fallen into the river which flowed past the town.
Gerda Oh, what long, dreary winter days those were!

Sunshine enters

Act II, The Snow Queen

Sunshine Then came the Sunshine and the warmer spring.
Gerda Kay is dead and gone!
Sunshine I don't think so, the Sunshine said in reply.

Sunshine exits

Gerda Kay is dead and gone! She said to the Swallows.

Some of the Chorus use their bodies, especially their hands, to manipulate themselves into swallows

Swallows We don't think so, answered the Swallows.
Gerda And at last little Gerda did not think so either. I will put on my new red shoes——
Narrator 50 She said one morning ...
Gerda — those which Kay has never seen, and I will go down to the river and ask it about him.
Narrator 50 It was still early. She left a note for her Old Grandmother——

Gerda takes a note from her pocket and kisses the note. The Chorus make a kissing sound. Gerda posts the note into one of the blocks. Then, she takes a pair of red shoes from out of a block and puts them on

Narrator 50 And having put on the red shoes, she went out at the city gates, all alone, and down ——
Chorus — to the river.

Other members of the Chorus move DS to form a river

Gerda (*to the river*) Is it true that you have taken my little playfellow? I will give you my red shoes if you will give Kay back to me.
Narrator 50 It seemed to her as if the waves nodded in a peculiar way.

The River nods in a peculiar way

Gerda And then she took her red shoes, the things she liked best, and threw them both into the river. (*She throws her red shoes*)
Chorus Agh!
Narrator 50 But they fell near the side, and were washed on land again.

The River returns the shoes to Gerda

Chorus (*with relief*) Aaah!

Gerda It was exactly as if the river would not take what was so dear to her.
Chorus For it had not little Kay to give in return.
Gerda But she thought she had not thrown the shoes out far enough, so she got into a boat — (*she takes a rectangular shaped block, places it beside the river and steps into it*) which was there amongst the rushes, and threw the shoes into the water again.
Chorus Agh!
Narrator 51 Now the boat was not fastened, and the motion she caused in it drove it off from the land. It drifted out fast into the river.
Gerda Then little Gerda was frightened and began to cry
1st Swallow But no-one heard her except the Swallows.
2nd Swallow And they could not carry her to land.
1st Swallow So they flew along the banks, singing.
2nd Swallow As if to console her.
Swallows (*singing*) Here we are! Here we are!
Narrator 50 The boat glided down the stream.
Gerda And little Gerda sat there quite quiet, in her bare feet.
Chorus Whilst her little red shoes floated after her.
Gerda Perhaps the river will carry me to little Kay, she thought; and then she grew more cheerful. She stood up — (*she does so*) and for hours she admired the beautiful green banks.
Narrator 52 At length she came to a large orchard full of cherry-trees —

The Chorus form the cherry-trees and, using various blocks, the Enchantress's house

— in which there stood a little house with strange red and blue windows.

The Enchantress enters, carrying a stick and wearing a large hat

Enchantress And from out of the house came an old, a very old, woman, supporting herself on a hooked stick.
Narrator 52 She wore a large straw hat, painted all over with the most beautiful flowers.
Enchantress You poor little child!, the old woman said. How did you get on to the rushing stream and carried out into the world? And she walked right out into the river. (*She walks into the river*)
Chorus Splosh ... splosh ... splosh
Enchantress Caught hold of the boat with her stick — (*she catches the boat with her stick*) and having drawn it to land, lifted little Gerda out (*She lifts Gerda out*)
Narrator 52 Gerda was delighted to feel herself on dry land again.
Gerda Though a little bit frightened of the strange old woman.

Act II, The Snow Queen

Enchantress Come and tell me who you are and how you came here.
Gerda And Gerda told her all.
Enchantress The old woman shook her head — and mumbled ... Hem! Hem!
Gerda And when Gerda asked her whether she had seen little Kay ——
Enchantress She said that he had not passed yet, but that he would be sure to come and that therefore she must not be sad. Come and taste the cherries, and look at the flowers, which are more beautiful than any picture book.
Narrator 53 She then took Gerda by the hand and having led her into the house ——
Enchantress — locked the door.
Gerda Gerda began to eat the most delicious cherries ——
Enchantress — while the old woman combed her hair with a golden comb (*She combs Gerda's hair*) I have always longed to have a dear little girl like you, the old woman said, and you shall see how happily we get on together.
Gerda As she combed Gerda's hair, the little girl more and more forgot her playfellow Kay.
Enchantress For the old woman practised magic.
Narrator 53 But she was not a wicked witch.
Enchantress And only conjured a little just for her own amusement.
Narrator 53 And she wished to keep Gerda with her.
Enchantress On this account she went into the garden ——

The Chorus produce multi-coloured handkerchiefs, some red, and thereby form the garden. The Enchantress goes into the garden

—— and touching all the rose-trees with her stick, they sank down into the black earth.

As the Enchantress touches each of the red handkerchiefs, they sink and die

Narrator 53 So that there was no trace left of where they once had stood.
Enchantress The old woman was afraid that when Gerda saw the rose trees she might think of her own, and remembering little Kay, run away.

The Enchantress exits

Gerda goes into the flower garden

Gerda Gerda then came into the flower garden. Oh!
Chorus What a perfume!
Gerda And what splendour!
Narrator 54 There were all imaginable flowers of every season of the year, so that no picture book could be prettier. Gerda was delighted.

Gerda And played till the sun went down behind the high cherry-trees, when she slept and dreamed as delightfully as any queen on her wedding day. (*She sleeps*)
Chorus The next day ...

Gerda wakes and plays amongst the flowers

Gerda Gerda again played amongst the flowers in the warm sunshine.
Narrator 54 And thus many days passed by.
Gerda Gerda knew every flower, but as many as there were, it seemed to her as if one were missing, though she did not know which.
Narrator 54 Now, one day, she was sitting looking at the old woman's painted hat, and just the most beautiful of the flowers was a rose.
Gerda What! Are there no roses here?
Narrator 55 She looked in all the flower beds, but none was to be found.
Gerda And then she sat down and cried.
Chorus Now ——
Narrator 55 — it so happened that her tears fell on one of the spots where a rose tree was buried, and as the warm tears watered the ground ——

There is rising music. A rose tree rises up from one of the blocks

Rose-Tree — the tree sprang up in as full and beautiful blossom as it had ever been.
Gerda Gerda threw her arms around it, and kissed the roses (*She kisses each rose*)
Chorus And thought of her own rose-tree at home.
Gerda And of little Kay. (*To the Rose-Tree*) Oh, how I have been delayed! I came to look for Kay. Do you know where he is? Do you think he is dead?
Rose-Tree He is not dead, the Rose-Tree said, for I have been in the earth, where all the dead are, but Kay was not there.
Gerda Thank-you ...
Chorus Gerda said.
Gerda My poor Old Grandmother! She is no doubt longing for me, and is sad about me, as she was about Kay. But I will soon be back home, and bring Kay with me.
Narrator 56 And she ran in her bare feet, out into the wide world. She looked back ...

The Chorus approach Gerda

Chorus One ...

Gerda looks back

Two ...

Gerda looks back

Three ———

Gerda looks back

Narrator 56 — times, but there was no-one following her.
Gerda When she could run no longer she seated herself upon a large stone. (*She sits*)
Narrator 56 And, looking round her, she saw that summer was ———
Chorus — gone.
Narrator 56 It was late in the autumn.
Gerda Oh, goodness, how long I have delayed! Why, it has grown to autumn!
Chorus (*singing*) Cruelty has a human heart,
        Jealousy a human face,
        Terror, the human form divine,
        And Secrecy, the human dress.
        [*William Blake*]

There is a lighting change

The Prince and the Princess

It starts to snow

Narrator 57 Opposite where she was sitting ———

A Wild Raven enters

Wild Raven — a large, Wild Raven was hopping about on the snow. It had been watching her some time, shaking its head, and now it cried, Caw! Caw! How do? How do? It could not express itself better, but meant kindly toward the little girl, and asked, where are you going all alone in the wide world?
Gerda Gerda felt how much there lay in that one word! Alone. Then she told her whole story and asked the Raven, have you not seen Kay?
Wild Raven The Raven nodded quite knowingly and said, it may be, it may be!
Gerda What! You think you may have seen him?, the little girl cried, and hugged the Raven. (*She hugs the Wild Raven*)

Wild Raven So that she nearly squeezed him to death. Gently, gently! I think I know; I think it may have been little Kay; but, for certain, by now the princess has driven you out of his thoughts.
Gerda Does he live with a princess?
Wild Raven I understand what you say, but I find it difficult to express myself in your language. If you understand the raven's language, it will go better.
Gerda No, I never learned that. But my grandmother knew it. Oh, had I but learned it!
Wild Raven It does not matter. I will tell the story as well as I can, though it will be badly done.
Chorus Then the Raven told his story.
Wild Raven In this kingdom in which you are now lives a princess, who is so unbelievably clever. She has read, you see, all the newspapers that are in the world; read and forgotten them again, so clever is she. Lately, she was sitting on her throne, which is said not to be too comfortable, when she suddenly asked, "Why should I not marry?" So, she determined to get married; but she must have a husband who knew how to answer when spoken to; not one who could only stand there and look grand, for that is too stupid. You may believe every word I say, for I have a tame sweetheart who wanders at liberty all over the palace, and it was she who has told me all this.
Narrator 57 The sweetheart was ——
Chorus —— of course ——
Narrator 57 —— a raven as well.
Wild Raven And so there appeared a fine stream of good-looking young men, pushing and shoving, outside the palace gates. But none of them succeeded, either on the first or the second day. They could speak well enough out in the street, but when they got into the palace and saw the guards in silver, and the stairs lined with footmen in gold, and saw the splendid rooms, they were quite bewildered. So when they stood before the throne on which the princess sat, they could say nothing more than repeat the last word she had uttered, and that she did not particularly care about hearing again.
Gerda But Kay! Little Kay! When did he come?
Wild Raven Patience!
Gerda Was he amongst the crowd?
Wild Raven Patience! We are just coming to him. It was on the third day, there came a little person without horse or carriage, but walking merrily straight up to the palace. His eyes were bright like yours, and he was very handsome, but also poorly dressed.
Gerda That was Kay! At last I have found him!

Act II, The Snow Queen

Wild Raven That's as may be. Nonetheless, my tame sweetheart tells me the boy walked straight up to the princess, who was sitting on a pearl as large as a spinning wheel, and not in the least abashed, he said that he had not come at all to pay court to the princess but only to hear how clever she was.
Gerda Oh, for certain that was Kay, for he was always so clever. Will you not introduce me into the palace?
Wild Raven Well, that is easily said, but how are we to manage it? I must talk it over with my tame sweetheart, and she will no doubt be able to advise us. I must tell you that a little girl like you will never obtain permission to enter in the ordinary way.
Gerda Oh, yes I shall, for as soon as Kay hears that I am there, he will come out directly and fetch me.
Narrator 57 The Raven wagged its head.

The Wild Raven wags his head

Wild Raven Wait for me there at the railing ——
Narrator 57 — and flew off

The Wild Raven exits

The raven did not return until late in the evening, when it said ...

The Wild Raven returns, carrying a loaf of bread

Wild Raven She sends you all sorts of kind messages, and here is a small loaf for you — *(he gives the loaf to Gerda)*, which she took from the kitchen, where there is plenty of it, and no doubt you are hungry. It is impossible for you to be admitted into the palace, for you are without shoes. The guards in silver and the footmen in gold would never allow it; but do not cry, for get in you shall. My sweetheart knows a little back staircase, which leads up to the bedroom, and she knows where to find the key.
Chorus So ——
Narrator 57 — they went into the garden ——
Chorus — into the great avenue ——
Narrator 57 — and when the lights in the palace were put out ——

The lighting darkens

— the Raven led Gerda to a back-door, which stood ajar.

The Chorus begin a ghostly wailing

Gerda Oh, how Gerda's heart beat with fear, and, at the same time, with delight.

Narrator 57 They were now on the stairs, where a small lamp was burning.

The Tame Raven enters carrying a lamp

Tame Raven And on the landing stood the Tame Raven, turning her head first on one side ... (*She does so*)
Chorus Caw!
Tame Raven And then on the other... (*She does so*)
Chorus Caw!
Tame Raven And then looked at Gerda. (*She does so*)
Chorus CAW!!

Gerda curtsies

Gerda Who curtsied as her grandmother had taught her to do.
Tame Raven My future husband has spoken to me so much in your praise, and your story, too, is very touching. If you, my little lady, will please to take the lamp ... (*She gives Gerda the lamp*), I will lead the way. We are going the straight way, for there we shall not meet anyone.

Gerda, the Wild Raven and the Tame Raven continue their journey

Gerda It seems to me as if someone were coming just behind us.

The wailing swells

It was like shadows on the wall, horses with flowing manes and thin legs, huntsmen, and ladies and gentlemen on horseback.
Tame Raven Those are only dreams, and come to carry the ladies' and gentlemen's thoughts off to the hunt.
Narrator 57 Each room they passed through was more splendid than the one before.

The wailing swells again

The dreams rushed pass them again, but went so fast that Gerda could not catch a sight of them.
Chorus And now they reached the bedroom.
Narrator 57 The ceiling was like large palm leaves made of the most beautiful glass. And there were two beds in the form of lilies.

The Prince and Princess enter. The Prince holds a large red sheet and the Princess holds a large white sheet which prevent them from being seen. The sheets represent their separate beds

Act II, The Snow Queen 37

One was white.

Gerda looks at the Prince and Princess

Gerda And in that lay the princess.
Narrator 57 The other was red.
Gerda And in that Gerda was to look for little Kay. (*She looks inside the red bed*) Oh, it is Kay! (*Calling to Kay*) Kay!

The wailing swells once again

Narrator 57 The dreams rushed back out of the room. He awoke ...
Chorus But ...

The Prince appears from behind the sheet

Prince My name isn't Kay!

The Princess appears from behind the sheet

Princess At the same time the princess's face appeared amongst the white lily-leaves. (*To Gerda*) What is the matter?
Gerda Little Gerda then cried and told her whole story, and all that the ravens had done for her.
Prince ⎫
Princess ⎭ (*together*) Poor child!
Princess And they praised the ravens for what they had done.
Prince And promised them a reward.
Princess (*to the Ravens*) Will you go free? Or will you have a fixed appointment as Court-Ravens?
Narrator 57 The two Ravens made their bows ——

The Ravens bow

—— and begged they might have a fixed appointment, for they thought of their old age, saying ...
Wild Raven ⎫
Tame Raven ⎭ (*together*) It is so nice to have something for the old age.
Narrator 57 Gerda then thought:
Gerda How good men and beasts are!

During the following, the Prince and Princess clothe Gerda in their red and white sheets, representing her red velvet dress and her white silk shawl

Chorus *(singing)* Mercy has a human heart,
Pity a human face,
And Love, the human form divine,
And Peace, the human dress.
[*William Blake*]

Narrator 57 The next day Gerda was clothed from head to foot in silk and velvet.
Prince Which she received.
Princess And she also received the offer to remain at the palace.
Prince And enjoy herself.
Gerda But Gerda only asked for a pair of boots.

The Tame Raven takes off her boots and gives them to Gerda

Tame Raven Which she received. Farewell, the Tame Raven said.
Prince Farewell!
Princess Farewell!
Prince The prince ——
Princess — and princess said.
Gerda Whilst little Gerda cried.
Wild Raven And the Wild Raven cried too.
Narrator 58 The Wild Raven escorted her for the first ten miles of her journey.
Wild Raven And then the Raven had to say farewell, which was the saddest parting of all.

The Wild Raven, Prince and Princess exit

Narrator 58 He flew up into a tree, and flapped his wings for as long as he could see her.

There is a lighting change

The Little Robber Girl

Narrator 59 After she had travelled many more miles ...
Gerda Gerda found herself ——
Chorus — in a great forest——
Narrator 59 Where — she was set upon ...
Chorus Agh!

A Robber Woman enters

Act II, The Snow Queen

Robber Woman By an old Robber Woman. The girl is nice, the girl is fat, the girl has been fed upon nuts.
Narrator 59 The old Robber Woman said.
Robber Woman She had a long bristly beard, and eyebrows which hung down over her eyes. (*Of Gerda*) Why, she is as good as a fat lamb! How nice she will taste! And she then drew out her long knife (*She draws a knife*)
Narrator 59 Which shone so that it was horrible to look at.

The Robber Girl enters and jumps on the Robber Woman's back. She bites the ear of the woman

Chorus Ow!
Robber Woman Ow!
Narrator 59 The old woman cried, for she had been bitten on the ear by her own daughter.
Robber Girl Who was so wild and wicked that nothing could be done with her.
Robber Woman You hateful imp! The old woman cried. Now, I haven't the time to kill this little girl.
Robber Girl Good, for she shall play with me; and she shall give me her beautiful silk, her beautiful velvet and her beautiful boots. Then she bit her mother again.
Chorus Agh!

The Robber Girl bites her mother again

Robber Woman Ow! And the old woman in return flipped her on the nose (*She does so*)
Robber Girl Ow!
Robber Woman But that was from sheer love.

The Robber Woman exits

Robber Girl The little Robber Girl was as tall as Gerda, but stronger, with broader shoulders and a dark skin. Her eyes were black, and she had a rather melancholy expression.
Narrator 60 She laid hold of Gerda round the waist and said ...
Robber Girl She shall not kill you, as long as I am not angry with you! You are a princess, I suppose?
Gerda No.
Narrator 60 Gerda said.
Gerda And told her all that she had undergone, and how much she loved little Kay.

Narrator 60 The Robber Girl looked at her quite seriously, nodded her head slightly, and said ...
Robber Girl She shall not kill you, even if I am angry with you. But I'll do it myself then.
Narrator 60 She dried Gerda's eyes.
Robber Girl And then put on the silken shawl —— (*She does so*)
Chorus Aaaah!
Robber Girl —— the velvet skirt —— (*She does so*)
Chorus Aaaah!
Robber Girl —— and the beautiful boots. (*She does so*)
Chorus Aaaaaaaaaaaaahhh!!
Narrator 61 The robber's castle was all in ruins, and the ravens and crows flew out of the holes. The girl led Gerda into the large, old, smoke-coloured hall.

Some of the Chorus form a hall using various building blocks

The lighting changes. Gerda and the Robber Girl walk DS, *entering the hall. Simultaneously, Bae and the Wood Pigeons step forward from the Chorus. The Wood Pigeons hold two pieces of wood vertically in front of themselves, thereby forming their "cages"*

Robber Girl Here, behind these bars, there are two Wood Pigeons that would fly away directly if they were not properly secured. And here stands my dear old Bae!
Narrator 61 As she said this, she pulled forward an old reindeer ——
Bae —— who was fastened by a bright copper ring it had around its neck.
Robber Girl We have to keep him a prisoner too, or he would be off. Every evening I tickle his throat with my sharp knife which frightens him dreadfully. (*She draws her knife*)
Narrator 61 The little girl then drew a long knife out.
Robber Girl And let it glide across the reindeer's throat. (*She does so*)
Bae Which made the poor beast tremble and shake.
Robber Girl But let me hear again what you said about little Kay, and why you came into the wide world.
Gerda And Gerda told all again from the beginning.
Narrator 61 And the Wood Pigeons fluttered in their cage, saying:
Chorus Coo! Coo!
Wood Pigeons We have seen little Kay. We have seen little Kay.
1st Wood Pigeon The Snow Queen took him away in her beautiful carriage.
2nd Wood Pigeon Which drove close over the forest as we lay in our nest.
1st Wood Pigeon She blew upon us young ones.
2nd Wood Pigeon And all excepting us two died.

Act II, The Snow Queen

Chorus Coo! Coo!
Gerda What are you saying? Where was the Snow Queen going to? Do you know anything about it?
1st Wood Pigeon She was most likely going to the North Pole.
2nd Wood Pigeon For there is always snow and ice up there.
1st Wood Pigeon Ask Bae the reindeer; he's sure to know.
Chorus Coo! Coo!
Bae There is ice and snow, and there it is also delightful and healthy. There one can jump and run about. (*He jumps and runs about*) And there the Snow Queen has her palace, on the island which is called ... (*He thinks very hard*) Spitzbergen.
Gerda Oh, Bae! My dear little Kay!
Robber Girl (*to Bae*) I might still have a good deal of fun, tickling you with the sharp knife — but then you are very old. I will unfasten you, and let you out, so that you may run to the North Pole. But you must make good use of your old legs, and carry this little girl to the Snow Queen's palace, where her playfellow is.
Gerda Gerda cried with joy.
Robber Girl I won't have you blubbering, for then you look exactly like my ugly mother. And the silk, and the velvet and the boots I shall keep, for they are so pretty. But here is a loaf, so you will not die of hunger. (*To Bae*) Now run, but take good care of the little girl.
Gerda Gerda stretched out her hand towards the Robber Girl and cried, farewell!
Robber Girl Puh!

The Robber Girl exits

Narrator 62 And the reindeer flew as fast as possible through the great forest, and over heaths and marshes.

Bae and Gerda exit

It flew day and night. Until, at last, it carried little Gerda to the island of Spitzbergen, and to the gates of the Snow Queen's palace.

The Chorus, except Narrator 62, begin to exit during the following. As they exit they take all the wooden building blocks, leaving the stage completely empty

Chorus (*singing*) Cruelty has a human heart,
              Jealousy a human face
              Terror, the human form divine,
              And Secrecy, the human dress.
              [*William Blake*]

Narrator 62 But let us now go inside the Snow Queen's palace, and see what little Kay was going.

He exits

The lighting changes

The Snow Queen's Palace

Narrator 63 enters

Narrator 63 The palace walls ——

Narrator 64 enters

Narrator 64 — were of driven snow.
Narrator 63 And the doors and windows ——
Narrator 64 — of the cutting winds.
Narrator 63 There were more than a hundred rooms, as the snow had formed them, and all were lighted by the bright northern light.
Narrator 64 They were all so large, so empty, and so icy-cold and shining.
Narrator 63 There was never any amusement here.
Narrator 64 Not even a game of cards, with tea and scandal.
Narrator 63 But empty, vast, and cold, were the rooms in the Snow Queen's palace.
Narrator 64 In the middle of the largest snow-room there was a frozen lake.
Narrator 63 Cracked into a thousand pieces.
Narrator 64 But each piece so like the others that it appeared a master-work of art.
Narrator 63 ⎫
Narrator 64 ⎭ (*together*) And in the middle of this stood ——

The Snow Queen enters

Snow Queen — the Snow Queen. When she was at home. She used to say that she then stood in the mirror of reason, and that it was the only one in the world.

Kay enters pulling a long length of white rope. As the narration continues, he traverses the stage, connecting the rope to the stage's extremities and thereby forms an enormous geometrical conundrum. Or is it a Cat's Cradle? Or is it the ice of the Snow Queen's Palace itself?

Narrator 64 Little Kay was quite blue with cold.

Act II, The Snow Queen

Narrator 63 Indeed — almost black.
Kay But he did not know it.
Snow Queen For she had kissed away the frost-shiver and his heart was like a lump of ice.
Narrator 64 Kay was dragging some sharp-edged, flat pieces of ice about.
Narrator 63 Just as we do with small pieces of wood when making a jig-saw puzzle.
Kay Kay was forming figures of the most wonderful description, and that was the ice-game of the understanding.
Narrator 64 In his eyes the figures were perfect.
Narrator 63 And of the highest importance.
Narrator 64 For the piece of glass which was in his eye made him think this.
Narrator 63 He formed whole words.
Narrator 64 But he could never succeed in the one word he wished to have. The word ——
Snow Queen — Eternity.
Narrator 64 For the Snow Queen had said to him:
Snow Queen If you can succeed in forming that one word you shall be your own master. And I will give you the whole world, together with a new pair of skates.
Kay But he could not.
Snow Queen I am now going to pay a visit to the warmer countries, and intend giving a peep into the black cauldrons.
Narrator 63 She meant the volcanoes Etna ——
Narrator 64 — and Vesuvius.
Snow Queen I will cover them with white; which will also do away with the orange-trees and vines.
Narrator 64 The Snow Queen then flew away.

The Snow Queen flies away

Kay And Kay was left alone in those vast empty rooms, staring at the pieces of ice, and thinking and thinking, till his brain almost cracked. (*He sits with his head in his hands*)
Narrator 63 He sat there quite stiff and still.
Narrator 64 So that it appeared as if he were frozen.

Gerda enters

Gerda Just then little Gerda came through the large gate into the palace. (*She journeys through the enormous Cat's Cradle*) And she saw Kay.
Narrator 63 She recognized him at once.
Narrator 64 And ran up to him.

Gerda runs up to Kay

Narrator 63 And pressed him closely to her.

Gerda does so

Narrator 64 And cried——
Gerda Kay! Dear little Kay! I have found you at last!
Kay But Kay sat quite still, stiff and cold.
Gerda And little Gerda cried.
Narrator 63 Bitter, burning tears.
Narrator 64 Which fell upon his breast.
Narrator 63 And, penetrating to his heart, thawed the lump of ——
Narrator 63
Narrator 64 } *(together)* — ice.
Narrator 64 And dissolved the piece of broken ——
Narrator 63
Narrator 64 } *(together)* — glass.
Kay He looked at her. (*He does so*)
Gerda She looked at him. (*She does so*)
Kay
Gerda } *(together)* And they sang ——
  (*Singing*)   The rose blooms,
Narrator 63
Narrator 64 } *(joining in; singing)*
         But its glory past,

Narrator 65 and Narrator 66 enter

Narrator 65
Narrator 66 } *(joining in; singing)*
         Christmas then approaches fast.
Kay Kay then burst into tears.
Narrator 65 And cried till the pieces of glass were washed out of his eyes.
Narrator 66 Then he recognized Gerda, and exclaimed in delight:
Kay Gerda? Dear little Gerda! Where have you been all this time? And where have I been?
Narrator 65 He looked all around, and continued ——
Kay How cold it is here! And how vast and empty!
Narrator 66 He pressed closely to her.

Kay presses himself close to Gerda

Gerda And she laughed and cried in turns.

Act II, The Snow Queen

Narrator 65 There was such joy that even the pieces of ice sang ——

The Chorus enter, singing. Some members of the Chorus disconnect the rope and use it, and their bodies, to form the word "Eternity" as the song finishes

Chorus   He doth give his joy to all,
He becomes an infant small.
He becomes a man of woe,
He doth feel the sorrow too.

Think not though canst sigh a sigh,
And thy maker is not by;
Think not thou canst weep a tear
And thy maker is not near.

Oh, he gives to us his joy
That our grief he may destroy;
Till our grief is fled and gone,
He doth sit by us and moan.
[*William Blake*]

Kay And when they were tired, the pieces of ice stood still and formed the letters of the word ——
Chorus Eternity.
Kay So that Kay was now his own master.
Gerda Gerda kissed his cheek. (*She does so*)
Kay And the colour came back into them.
Gerda She kissed his eyes. (*She does so*)
Kay And they were as bright as her own.
Gerda She kissed his hands. (*She does so*)
Kay And he was himself again. But the Snow Queen might return at any moment.
Chorus Aaaaagghh!

The members of the Chorus forming the letters of the word "Eternity" exit

Gerda So they took each other by the hand.

Kay and Gerda take each other by the hand

Kay And ran out of the palace.

They run out of the palace and exit

Narrator 67 And the sun burst forth.
Chorus It was spring!
Narrator 68 With green leaves.
Narrator 67 And beautiful flowers.
Narrator 68 The church bells rang.

The remaining members of the Chorus make the sound of church bells ringing

Narrator 67 And they recognized the high steeples.
Narrator 68 And the large city.
Chorus It was that in which they lived!
Narrator 67 So they entered it.
Narrator 68 And went straight to their old houses.
Chorus Where the flowers were in full bloom.

The Chorus pull out coloured handkerchiefs to form flowers in full bloom

Old Grandmother enters with a bible

Old Grandmother The grandmother walked in the clear sunshine, and read aloud out of the bible. (*Reading from the bible*) Whosoever shall not receive the kingdom of God as a little child, shall in no wise enter heaven.
Narrator 66 Then Kay and Gerda entered the garden
Chorus But ——

Adult Kay and Adult Gerda enter. Adult Gerda holds the box of the Little Match Girl

— they were no longer children.
Adult Kay And there stood Kay ——
Adult Gerda — and Gerda.
Adult Kay Hand in hand.
Adult Gerda Grown up.
Adult Kay And yet still children.
Adult Gerda For in their hearts they were children.
Adult Kay And it was summer.
Adult Gerda Warm ——
Adult Kay — delightful ——
Chorus — Summer.

Gerda throws rose petals out of the box over them. All sing

Company Mercy has a human heart,
Pity a human face,
And Love, the human form divine,
And Peace, the human dress.
[*William Blake*]

THE END

FURNITURE AND PROPERTY LIST

ACT I
THE LITTLE MATCH GIRL

On stage: Coloured life-sized children's wooden building blocks; various shapes and sizes. *In them*: soldiers' muskets, piece of rope

Off stage: Wooden box containing matches and tin soldiers (**The Little Match Girl**)
Large slipper (**Boy**)

THE BRAVE TIN SOLDIER

On stage: No additional props required

Personal: **First Boy**: paper

ACT II
THE SNOW QUEEN

On stage: Coloured life-sized children's wooden building blocks; various shapes and sizes. *In them*: rose-trees on a bunting line, paper snow, red shoes, rose-tree, two pieces of wood
Rectangular piece of rope

Off stage: Sleigh (**Snow Queen**)
Stick (**Enchantress**)
Loaf of bread (**Wild Raven**)
Lamp (**Tame Raven**)
Large red sheet (**Prince**)
Large white sheet (**Princess**)
Knife (**Robber Woman**)
Knife (**Robber Girl**)
Long length of white rope (**Kay**)
Bible (**Old Grandmother**)
Wooden box containing rose petals (**Adult Gerda**)

Personal: **Narrator 31**: spectacles
Kay: half-penny, magnifying-glass
Gerda: half-penny, note
Grandmother: comb
Narrators 38 and **39**: paper snow
Chorus: multi-coloured handkerchiefs, some red; paper snow

LIGHTING PLOT

Practical fittings required: nil

ACT I, THE LITTLE MATCH GIRL

To open: Exterior lighting; dusk, snow falling

Cue 1	**Chorus** members enter carrying lanterns *Covering spots on lanterns*	(Page 5)
Cue 2	All the **Chorus** exit *Bring lighting slowly up to winter morning effect*	(Page 7)
Cue 3	At the end of the song *Black-out*	(Page 8)

ACT I, THE BRAVE TIN SOLDIER

To open: General interior lighting

Cue 4	**Narrator 13**: " ... down into the street." *Exterior lighting; morning effect*	(Page 13)
Cue 5	**Chorus**: " It now began to rain." *Rain effect, increasing in intensity*	(Page 13)
Cue 6	**First Boy** steps out of the **Chorus** *Cut rain effect*	(Page 14)
Cue 7	The **Chorus** reform the nursery *Bring up interior lighting; flame effect on stove*	(Page 17)
Cue 8	At the end of the song *Black-out*	(Page 19)

ACT II, THE SNOW QUEEN

To open: General exterior lighting

Cue 9	**Chorus**: "Agh!" *Dim lighting, snow falling*	(Page 21)

Cue 9	**Chorus**: (*singing*) "... the human dress." *Lighting change*	(Page 22)
Cue 10	**Narrator 37**: " But in winter ——" *Dim lighting, snow falling*	(Page 23)
Cue 11	**Kay** and **Gerda** move up and down the stairs *Warm spot on Gerda and Kay*	(Page 23)
Cue 12	**Narrator 41**: "Then came spring." *Cut spot. Bring up spring morning effect*	(Page 25)
Cue 13	**Old Grandmother**: "... play with **Gerda**." *Fade to winter lighting, snow falling*	(Page 26)
Cue 14	**Chorus**: (*singing*) "... approaches fast." *Lighting change*	(Page 28)
Cue 15	**Sunshine** enters *Bring up spot on Sunshine*	(Page 28)
Cue 16	**Sunshine** exits *Cut spotlight*	(Page 29)
Cue 17	**Chorus**: (*singing*) "... the human dress." *Lighting change, snow falling*	(Page 33)
Cue 18	**Narrator 57**: " ... were put out ——" *The lighting darkens*	(Page 35)
Cue 19	**The Tame Raven** enters with a lamp *Covering spot on lamp*	(Page 36)
Cue 20	**Narrator 58**: " ... he could see her." *Lighting change*	(Page 38)
Cue 21	The **Chorus** form a hall *Lighting change*	(Page 40)
Cue 22	**Narrator 62** exits *Lighting change*	(Page 42)
Cue 23	**Adult Kay** and **Adult Gerda** enter *Bring up summer lighting effect*	(Page 46)

EFFECTS PLOT

The following effects plot is applicable if Tony Coffey's original score is not used. (Please see Music Notes on page viii and Author's Notes on page ix regarding music)

Act I

Cue 1	To open Act I *Music plays*	(Page 1)
Cue 2	**Narators 1, 2, 3** (*together*) " New Year's Eve." *Cut music*	(Page 2)
Cue 3	**Big Iron Stove**: " A big iron stove." *Bar of magical music*	(Page 4)
Cue 4	**Stage Right Wall/Stage Left Wall** (*together*): "— died." *Bar of disappointed music*	(Page 4)
Cue 5	**Chorus**: "—vanished." *Bar of disappointed music*	(Page 4)
Cue 6	**Little Match Girl**: " ... brighter than daylight." *Music*	(Page 6)
Cue 7	The **Chorus** stop humming *A fanfare plays*	(Page 8)
Cue 8	The **Boy** lines up the toy tin soldiers *A military drum and cornet play*	(Page 8)
Cue 9	**Chorus**: "... playthings began to play ..." *Music plays. Cacophanous sound of playthings:* *whipping tops and nutcracker (etc.)*	(Page 9)
Cue 10	**Whipping Top/Ball** (*together*) "...other no more." *Music plays. Cacophanous sound of playthings:* *whipping tops and nutcracker (etc.)*	(Page 10)
Cue 11	**Narrator 11**: " ... made of cardboard." *Music plays*	(Page 11)

Cue 12	**Brave Tin Soldier**: " ... from one instant.' *Music plays*	(Page 12)
Cue 13	The **Imp** vanishes into the block *Music plays*	(Page 13)
Cue 14	**Narrator 13**: " ... down into the street." *Falling music*	(Page 13)
Cue 15	**Chorus**: " Then the door flew open." *Music for* **Dancer,** *continue until end of Act*	(Page 18)

Act II

Cue 16	To begin Act II *Music plays*	(Page 20)
Cue 17	**Kay**: "You're making me feel cross." *Music for the entrance of the* **Snow Queen**	(Page 27)
Cue 18	**Narrator 55**: " ... watered the ground ——" *Rising music*	(Page 32)